TO:

FROM:

SLOTH WISDOM

Compiled by Talia Levy
and Jax Berman
Illustrated by Lindsay Dale

PETER PAUPER PRESS, INC.
White Plains, New York

To all the slow-movers
who like to hang out.

Designed by Margaret Rubiano

Illustrations © Lindsay Dale

Copyright © 2016
Peter Pauper Press, Inc.
202 Mamaroneck Avenue
White Plains, NY 10601
All rights reserved
ISBN 978-1-4413-1940-1
Printed in China
21 20 19
Visit us at www.peterpauper.com

SLOTH WISDOM

Take a hint from a sloth. Nobody would call them zippy, but swiftness isn't everything. Their measured, methodical approach to life has worked for millennia. They live in harmonic symbiosis with their environment. Sure, they're so slow that algae grows on them, but that serves them pretty well—their greenish coat lets them hide from predators among the foliage. They make their choices, from which leaves they'll munch to what branch they'll grasp next, with careful consideration. And of course, they get a lot of sleep. We humans tend to associate slowness and idleness with waste, but going slow can yield rich, surprising rewards. Let yourself lie fallow for a while. Next time you get a chance, squeeze in a nap. Take the time to consider things, and also allow your thoughts to wander without a goal in mind. You might discover something surprising about the world or yourself. Or you might just enjoy a really pleasant rest.

There's never
enough time to do
all the nothing
you want.

Bill Watterson,
Calvin and Hobbes

Slow down and enjoy life. It's not only the scenery you miss by going too fast—you also miss the sense of where you are going and why.

EDDIE CANTOR

Don't just
do something,
sit there.

Sylvia Boorstein

OF ALL THE THINGS A MAN
MAY DO, SLEEP PROBABLY
CONTRIBUTES MOST TO
KEEPING HIM SANE.

Roger Zelazny

Wisely and slowly; they stumble that run fast.

WILLIAM SHAKESPEARE

Rest is not idleness,
and to lie sometimes
on the grass under trees
on a summer's day,
listening to the murmur
of the water, or watching
the clouds float across
the sky, is by no means
a waste of time.

JOHN LUBBOCK

To the mind
that is still,
the whole universe
surrenders.

Laozi

We revel in
the laxness
of the path
we take.

Charles Baudelaire

Life moves
pretty fast. If you
don't stop and look
around once in
a while, you
could miss it.

FERRIS BUELLER

Never waste any time you can spend sleeping.

FRANK H. KNIGHT

I love deadlines. I love the whooshing noise they make as they go by.

DOUGLAS ADAMS

The more relaxed
you are, the better you are
at everything: the better you
are with your loved ones, the
better you are with your enemies,
the better you are at your
job, the better you are
with yourself.

Bill Murray

We should take a pillow wherever we go.

Dan Kiernan and Tom Hodgkinson

It's very important that
we re-learn the art of resting
and relaxing. Not only does
it help prevent the onset of
many illnesses that develop
through chronic tension
and worrying; it allows us
to clear our minds, focus,
and find creative solutions
to problems.

THÍCH NHẤT HẠNH

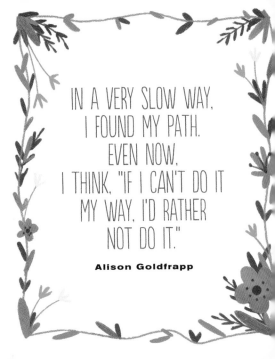

IN A VERY SLOW WAY,
I FOUND MY PATH.
EVEN NOW,
I THINK, "IF I CAN'T DO IT
MY WAY, I'D RATHER
NOT DO IT."

Alison Goldfrapp

I am a firm
believer that one
way to become
enlightened is to
be so relaxed,
as relaxed as you
possibly can be.

ALANIS MORISSETTE

Be the nap
you wish to see
in the world.

Patricia Robinson

The imagination
needs moodling—
long, inefficient,
happy idling, dawdling
and puttering.

BRENDA UELAND

Worry will never solve tomorrow's problems. It will only take energy away from today.

James Altucher

My passions are all asleep,
from my having slumbered till
nearly eleven, and weakened
the animal fiber all over me to a
delightful sensation about three
degrees on this side of faintness.
If I had teeth of pearl and
the breath of lilies I should call
it languor, but as I am
I must call it laziness.

John Keats

I suppose the secret of his success is in his tremendous idleness, which almost approaches the supernatural.

LAWRENCE DURRELL

Well, when you're relaxed, your mind takes you to the whole reality. There's no such thing as time when you're really relaxed. That's why meditation works.

SHIRLEY MACLAINE

There is
more to life than
simply increasing
its speed.

Mahatma Gandhi

I wake
to sleep, and
take my
waking slow.

Theodore Roethke

If you are
losing your
leisure, look out! —
It may be
you are losing
your soul.

VIRGINIA WOOLF

It's important to
slow down, every
now and then,
for no other
reason than to
call someone
to say hi.

SIMON SINEK

NO ONE CAN GET INNER PEACE BY POUNCING ON IT.

Harry Emerson Fosdick

I am happiest when I am idle. I could live for months without performing any kind of labor, and at the expiration of that time I should feel fresh and vigorous enough to go right on in the same way for numerous more months.

ARTEMUS WARD

WHEN YOU CAN'T
FIGURE OUT WHAT
TO DO, IT'S TIME
FOR A NAP.

Mason Cooley

You're only here
for a short visit.
Don't hurry, don't
worry. And be sure
to smell the flowers
along the way.

Walter Hagen

It is said that
nothing is impossible;
but there are lots
of people doing
nothing every day.

Theodor Rosyfelt

An unhurried
sense of time
is in itself a
form of wealth.

BONNIE FRIEDMAN

Lighthouses don't go running all over an island looking for boats to save; they just stand there shining.

Anne Lamott

Each person
deserves a day away
in which no problems are
confronted, no solutions
searched for. Each of
us needs to withdraw
from the cares which
will not withdraw
from us.

MAYA ANGELOU

One of the
symptoms of
an approaching
nervous breakdown
is the belief that
one's work is
terribly important.

Bertrand Russell

When action
grows unprofitable,
gather information;
when information
grows unprofitable,
sleep.

URSULA K. LE GUIN

Don't struggle about the struggle. In other words, life's full of ups and downs.

SEAN COVEY

WORK IS NOT
ALWAYS REQUIRED. . . .
THERE IS SUCH A THING
AS SACRED IDLENESS.

George MacDonald

It's not a man's working hours that are important—it's his leisure hours. That's the mistake we all make.

Agatha Christie

I worry about
the things I can
affect, and the
things I have no
control over
I move by.

Lenny Wilkens

Sleep is the consummate protection against the unseemliness that is the invariable consequence of being awake.

FRAN LEBOWITZ

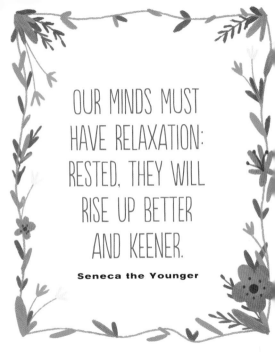

OUR MINDS MUST
HAVE RELAXATION:
RESTED, THEY WILL
RISE UP BETTER
AND KEENER.

Seneca the Younger

Though some choices
may slow our journey,
every path we take
gives us more familiarity
with how our actions
affect the world around
us, giving us more
opportunities to learn
how to help ourselves
and others.

MATTHEW UNDERWOOD

In philosophy
if you aren't
moving at a snail's
pace you aren't
moving at all.

IRIS MURDOCH

If you want to relax,
watch the clouds pass by
if you're laying on the grass,
or sit in front of the creek;
just doing nothing and
having those still
moments is what really
rejuvenates the body.

MIRANDA KERR

It's really important
to have balance, spend
some time in nature, go to
a few parties, enjoy my
friends and really
chill out.

Joakim Noah

I just refuse
to worry or get
upset or be fearful.
It doesn't do one
particle of good.

Paul Henderson

NEVER HURRY.
NATURE NEVER DOES.

John Lubbock

Life flies by, and it's easy to get lost in the blur.... I think the trick is living the questions. Not worrying so much about what's ahead but rather sitting in the gray area— being OK with where you are.

CHRIS PINE

Sleep is God.
Go worship.

Jim Butcher

Of all the free
pleasures out there
for the taking, the nap
is the easiest and
most satisfying.

DAN KIERNAN AND
TOM HODGKINSON

If a man insisted always on being serious, and never allowed himself a bit of fun and relaxation, he would go mad or become unstable without knowing it.

HERODOTUS

IT IS A
WONDERFUL
OPPORTUNITY,
THE POSSESSION
OF LEISURE.

E. M. Forster

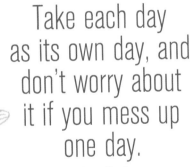

Take each day
as its own day, and
don't worry about
it if you mess up
one day.

Henry Cloud

My father taught
me to work, but not
to love it. I never did
like to work, and I don't
deny it. I'd rather read,
tell stories, crack jokes,
talk, laugh—anything
but work.

ABRAHAM LINCOLN

A lot of high-profile companies are recognizing the benefits of power napping.... It's like kindergarten all over again.

Stefanie Weisman

If a man does not keep pace with his companions, perhaps it is because he hears a different drummer. Let him step to the music which he hears, however measured or far away.

HENRY DAVID THOREAU

TO DO GREAT WORK
ONE MUST BE VERY IDLE
AS WELL AS VERY
INDUSTRIOUS.

Samuel Butler

It is requisite
for the relaxation
of the mind that
we make use,
from time to time,
of playful deeds
and jokes.

THOMAS AQUINAS

Be slow in
choosing a
friend, slower
in changing.

Benjamin Franklin

I can't live
my life worrying
about something
that might
never happen.

BILL PARCELLS

I count it as an absolute certainty that in paradise, everyone naps.

Tom Hodgkinson

A broad
margin of leisure
is as beautiful
in a man's life as
in a book. Haste
makes waste, no
less in life than in
housekeeping.

HENRY DAVID THOREAU

My philosophy is
to take one day at
a time. Tomorrow
is even out of
sight for me.

Bobby Darin

LEARN FROM YESTERDAY, LIVE FOR TODAY, LOOK TO TOMORROW, REST THIS AFTERNOON.

Charles M. Schulz

My philosophy is to take one day at a time. Tomorrow is even out of sight for me.

Bobby Darin

LEARN FROM
YESTERDAY, LIVE
FOR TODAY, LOOK TO
TOMORROW, REST THIS
AFTERNOON.

Charles M. Schulz